Sh*t Literary Siblings

Sh*t Literary Siblings

First published in 2022 by
HEADLINE PUBLISHING GROUP

1

Cataloguing in Publication Data is available from the British Library

Hardback ISBN 978 1 4722 9633 7

Typeset by Beau Merchant at Toy Soldier Creative

Printed and bound in Great Britain by Clays Ltd, Elcograf S.p.A.

Headline's policy is to use papers that are natural, renewable and recyclable products and made from wood grown in well-managed forests and other controlled sources. The logging and manufacturing processes are expected to conform to the environmental regulations of the country of origin.

HEADLINE PUBLISHING GROUP
An Hachette UK Company
Carmelite House
50 Victoria Embankment
London EC4Y 0DZ

www.headline.co.uk
www.hachette.co.uk

Dedicated to the also-rans, the second-raters,
the almost-but-not-quites

INTRODUCTION

What is the point of literature? At *The Fence*, we have asked this question many times, whether as a clever diversionary tactic in a highbrow conversation, where we're trying to conceal the fact that we never actually finished *Ulysses* – or as we threw Boris Johnson's inexorable comic novel *72 Virgins* out of the window of our fifth-floor office. Really, what is the point of literature?

We could answer that in a million ways – all deeply pretentious – but this is a book that will be much more comfortable in a stocking or resting on the cistern of a lavatory than on the comparative literature reading list at Goldsmiths. If you have picked it up hoping for complex literary theory, then we can only apologise. If you'd hoped for something referencing Baudrillard then we can only apologise. Please do feel free to write an irate letter to the *London Review of Books* by way of protest. And while we're at the business of apologies – please forgive us a little platitude as we answer our own question: a work of literature is a dream rendered in ink and paper.

It is our considered opinion that the classics have failed to properly represent the breadth of the human imagination. The truth is, of course, that most of our dreams are either ordinary, embarrassing or downright disturbing. They are rarely about beauty or truth but instead about turning up naked for your GCSE maths exam. They don't take place on Chesil Beach or Mars but on the upper deck of the N35 nightbus to Clapham Junction.

We view it like this: literature is more than adequately served with great, well-rounded, complex heroes and villains. But most people aren't like that. So this book is a chronicle of that silent, strange majority who have been overlooked by the corpus of the Western canon. It's a collection of the weird, the pedestrian, the uninteresting and the unpublishable. It is a list of those younger and elder siblings of the great figures who stalk the literary dreamscape, who, until now, were ever destined to linger in their shadows. We had a chance to give these shit literary siblings their moment in the sun, and here it is.

Sh*t Literary Siblings

1.Donna Quixote

Quiet and calm owner of a moderately successful La Mancha nail and beauty parlour.

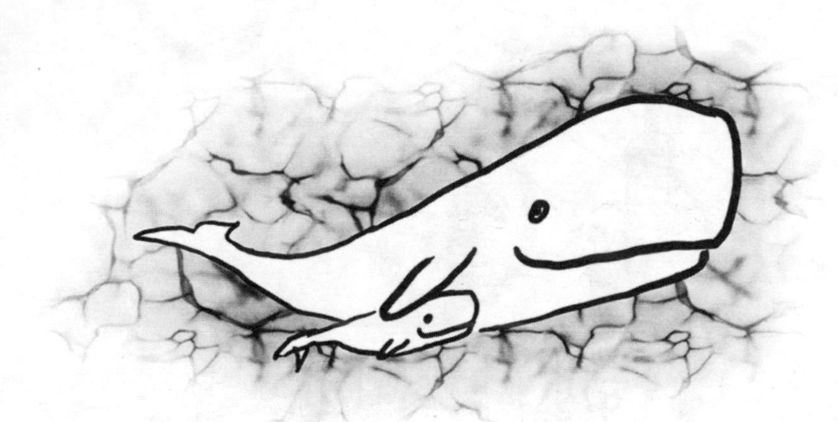

2. Moby Fanny

Sensible, no nonsense female whale who has raised several pods of young across the Pacific basin without once getting involved in any nonsense with a psychotic amputee.

3. Edna Baggins

Agoraphobic female Hobbit. Reliant on second breakfasts delivered by Uber Eats.

4. The Inept Mr Ripley

Credulous and bungling American holidaymaker serving a lengthy prison term for accidentally shoplifting a novelty fridge magnet from a kiosk at an Italian seaside resort.

SAN
REMO

5. Mr Zhivago

'Yes please little bro, do tell us all again about those six years in the Russian National Medical School for the Enigmatic but Handsome.'

6. Iphicle Poirot

A shy Belgian socialite, Iphicle was barred from most of polite society when it was revealed he had been murdering dinner guests and train passengers due to his social awkwardness. Announcing the murders to shocked attendees allowed him to deflect blame from himself and to quickly escape before any small talk was attempted.

7. Gerry Poppins

Armed robber. Wounded in an attempt to escape from Holloway Prison by jumping from the walls holding what he believed to be a talking umbrella.

8. Todd Gatsby

MAGA enthusiast and Alex Jones devotee. Owns an automobile dealership in Willingston, North Dakota.

9. Deirdre Bloom

No-nonsense Ranelagh housewife, homeschooling her children through their Leaving Certs.

10. Hayden Caulfield

Popular, gregarious and sexually active High School football captain.

11. Hugo Wooster

Currently berating his housemates for not cleaning the oven, after a long day manning the desk at Foxtons in Clapham High Street.

12. Wayne Jeeves

Slovenly commune resident and radical activist.
Occasional nudist.

13. Uncle Tim

Civil rights activist currently conducting zoom
masterclasses in peaceful protest from
his solar-powered office at the bottom of the garden.

14. The Cat in the Cone

Sickly, mute, drama averse feline.

15. Q. Alfred Prufrock

Former corporate accountant who upped sticks to go live on the Mexican coast. A man in love, he splits his time between his family and the crisp Pacific surf. Often wonders what he could have done to deserve all this happiness.

16. Anderson Crusoe

Chronically cautious traveller, much taken with uneventful caravan holidays and Midlands canal breaks.

17. Entirely Adequate Mr Fox

A perfectly fine woodland mammal, said by all to be highly capable of getting the job done. Not big on challenging farmers or commanding other creatures with charm and panache, more into sniffing round bins and picnic areas, that sort of thing.

18. Eleazar Scrooge

Conscientious and public minded Victorian employer and philanthropist who, after a series of supernatural encounters, becomes an enthusiast for the repeal of child labour legislation and the banning of trade unions.

19. Euston Bear

Peruvian caniform delivered to a less desirable London station. Now lives off Burger King wrapper sandwiches after his adoption by a group of kindly heroin addicts.

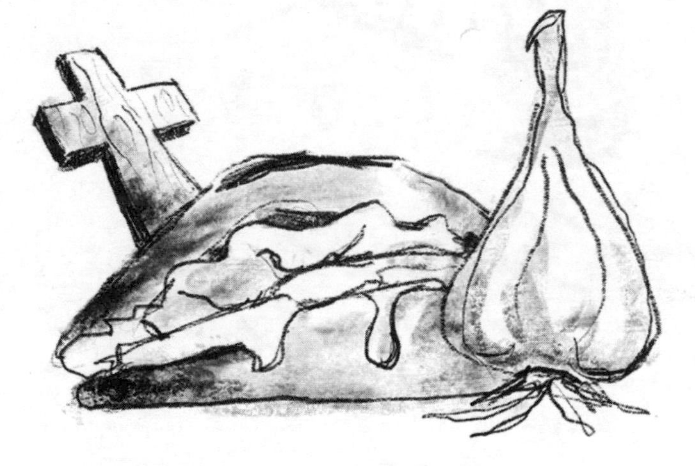

20. The Honourable Jeremy Dracula

Younger brother of the Count. Vegetarian – though would be vegan, if only he could resist sinking his fangs into a nice bit of halloumi. Local councillor for the Transylvania Lib Dems.

⚠ Check records

21. Hubert Humbert

Scout leader and community activist who finds that his DBS checks take much longer than they really should.

22. Gary Potter

Unremarkable 11-year-old boy referred to counselling services after butchering an owl with a penknife.

23. The Much Younger Brother Karamazov

Not as obsessed with discussing God, free will,
or the unspeakable cruelties of life, Dermot Karamazov
had a passion for Warhammer, building kit cars,
and currently works as assistant manager of the
Bromley branch of Halfords.

24. Claudia Dalloway

Operates a loss-making interior design company in Chelsea. Currently banned from both her daughters' Instagram accounts for commenting under every single photo.

25. The Unhappy Prince

Flint-hearted, handsy old fart, recently settled some court business for an undisclosed sum. His family aren't speaking to him.

26. Paul Pan

43-year-old tribal house DJ, currently living in a barge and holding raves for the idle west London elite.

27. Dick Galore

Long, long suffering sports correspondent for the Brighton Argus. Consistently overlooked for promotion. Bachelor. Goes by Richard.

28. Fyodor Samsa

Civil servant. Fast-stream success story and well-liked office presence. Awakes one day from uneasy dreams to discover he had been transformed into a guy posting photos of his weekend break to Lisbon on Facebook.

29. The Railway Adults

Anorak-clad, dandruff sufferers who linger in groups on the edges of mainline train routes and uncovered rural platforms. Too well versed in railway bylaws and local timetables to ever be hit by a train.

30. Gandalf the Greggs

Beardy, pastry-covered street wizard who spends long periods of time in the popular bakery chain. Will start talking to trees after a surfeit of sausage rolls.

31. The Tiger Who Came Too Quick

32. Peppi Longstocking

Hard-bitten and cynical Scandi child-detective investigating a series of horrific Moomin murders.

33. Walter Wonka

A Kettering dentist with a phobia of dwarves.

34. Sir Julian Falstaff

Thin and nervous male nanny. A teetotaller, he spends his free time tending his garden with his devoted 'life partner', Mr Eric Quickly.

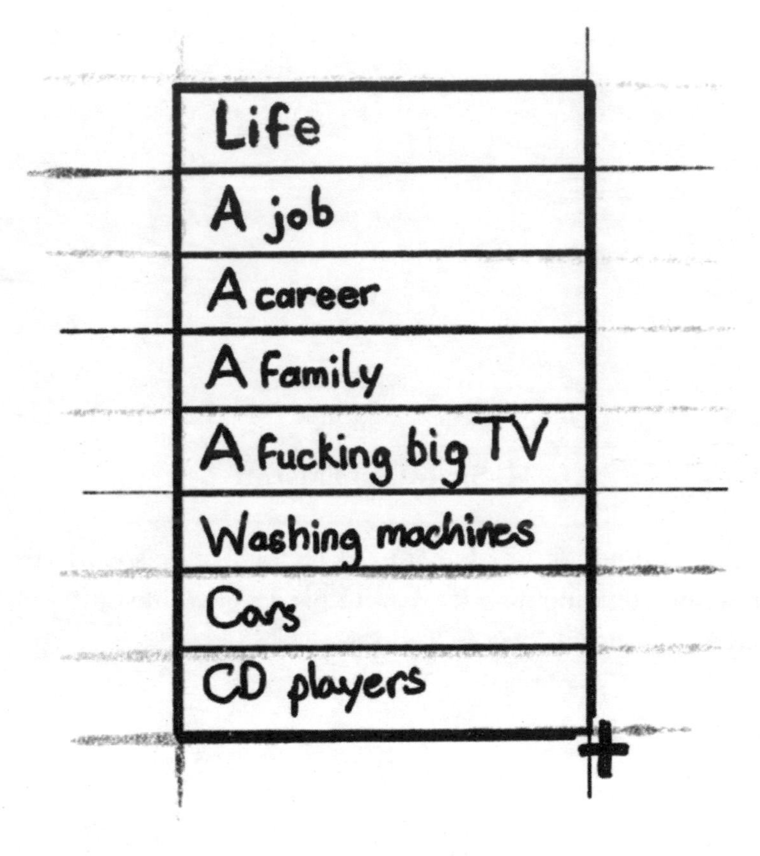

35. Mike Renton

A dour, Morningside-based tax accountant who sometimes – but only sometimes – treats himself to a second glass of sherry.

36. Hannah Karenina

Tells-it-like-it-is blonde whose massive social media following stems from her lewd behaviour on the syndicated show, 'The Real Housewives of Yasnaya Polyana'. Lives off sponsored Instagram posts advertising natural contraception apps.

37. Reginald of the Dump

Modern House fanatic who dreams of one day of living in a house designed by Berthold Lubetkin. Earned his ironic moniker by trawling the car boot sales of suburban London.

38. The Has Mental Health Issues and Is Working Through It Hatter

'You know what?' He takes a sip of chamomile tea. 'Sometimes you just *are* late for a very important date. And that's okay.'

39. Little Brother

Immature and out of his depth manchild who appears on screens at random intervals to unconvincingly tell the general public how to live their lives.

40. Molly Golightly

A parsimonious yoga teacher operating out in the Adirondacks, Molly won't be heading back to Manhattan anytime soon.

41. Stan of Green Gables

Obsessive and moody child from a small Canadian town who has an unhealthy relationship with a noted rap star.

42. Serge Smilé

Garrulous and amiable Parisian adulterer who routinely leaks state secrets over five-hour lunches in the 6th Arrondissement.

43. Pariah Heep

Washed-up bassist for noughties indie bands, loathed throughout the industry for tubthumping arrogance and grandiloquent pronouncements of genius.

44. Thursday Addams

Former Disney star who now runs an acai bowl stand in Venice Beach. Loves water paddling, her labrador Mikey and greeting everyone with a wide-eyed smile. Has far to go.

45. Mr Darcy QC, MP

Gawky lawyer with a good haircut. Women find him attractive until they hear his voice.

46. Mrs Havisham-Coutts

Married an insurance broker and lives in Notting Hill.
Hasn't seen sis for a while.

47. The Count of Montessori

Alfie, aged three, once slighted by his peers, has erected a world of vengeful intrigue in his local nursery.

48. Madame Ovary

Aspirant expat building her new post-Brexit life in Northern France. Moderates the comments on Mumsnet with no little fervour.

49. Stuart of Stuart Hall

Rambunctious critic of the state's monopoly and deployment of violence upon its subjects through a Marxist lens. Drives a tiny red car.

50. Gill Sikes

Charity worker and sex-workers' advocate. The single largest individual donor to Battersea Dogs Home.

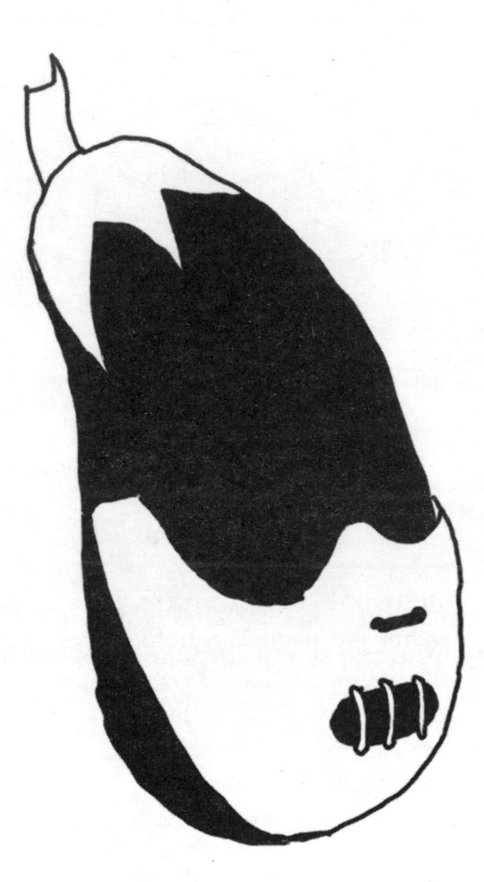

51. Annabelle Lecter

Natural wine advocate who runs a farm-to-table vegan supper club in a Hackney Wick industrial park.

52. Dorian Greer

Australian writer whose media profile remains unchanged even as her views get old before their time.

53. The Twats

A hideous and vindictive couple constantly seeking to screw each other over, using practical jokes, everyday cruelties, and columns in the national press.

54. Paul Bateman

A violent homicidal maniac who refuses to talk to his jailers and his psychiatrist about his condition.

55. Marshcliff and Carrie

Shabby, bog-wanking waft of a man trapped in a relationship with an ambitious young Catholic woman. Her torrid passion for posh curtains will destroy them both.

56. Christopher Batman

After losing both parents in a badger attack,
he trawls Hundred Acre Wood culling woodland
creatures every night.

57. Punnywise

Deeply tedious, self-proclaimed joker who lures people into his drain lair in order to bore them to death with wordplay dating from before the dawn of the universe.

58. Bi-Curious George

Adventurous monkey who wonders whether he'd enjoy a nibble on a banana.

59. Christopher Rabbit

Leftist firebrand turned sententious bore and latterly, neoconservative warmonger. Brother of widely respected Conservative columnist, Peter Rabbit.

60. The Robbers

Diminutive and surprisingly endearing individuals, who long ago graduated from merely borrowing. Their lifestyle is funded by liberating hub caps, copper wiring and multi packs of Carlsberg from their present owners.

61. Hadrian Mole, aged 1,884 and three quarters

Angsty, diary keeping Roman autarch.
Really, really insecure about the length of his wall
(he keeps measuring it).

62. Brigitte Jones

Home Counties publishing starlet made famous for her many lovers and bikini-clad photoshoots on the English riviera. Subsequently indicted on multiple counts of inciting racial hatred.

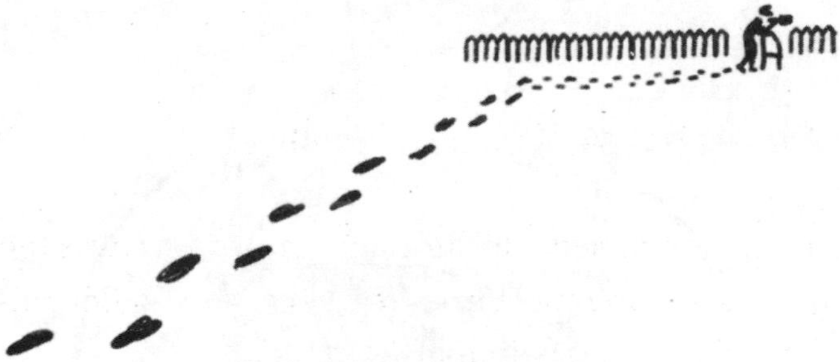

63. Sir Captain Nemo

Seemingly ageless junior officer unexpectedly knighted after being encouraged by his immediate family to walk twenty thousand leagues around his garden. Dies after a visit to the Mysterious Island (Barbados).

64. Albus Dimbleby

Revered, unmarried educator and wizard who was the second person to report from the liberation of Bergen-Belsen in 1945.

65. Ronan the Barbarian

Kerry-born, Dublin-based capitalist. His softly spoken manner hides a rapacious, red-in-tooth-and-claw capitalist who milked the Celtic Tiger for all it was worth. Domiciled in Panama for tax purposes.

66. Brew Radley

An extrovert IPA enthusiast resident in Brockley, will monologue about the bitter tartness of a sour beer at the drop of a hat.

67. Salt-Pig

Flamboyant, porcine Turk, globally renowned for his impeccably well-seasoned chops.

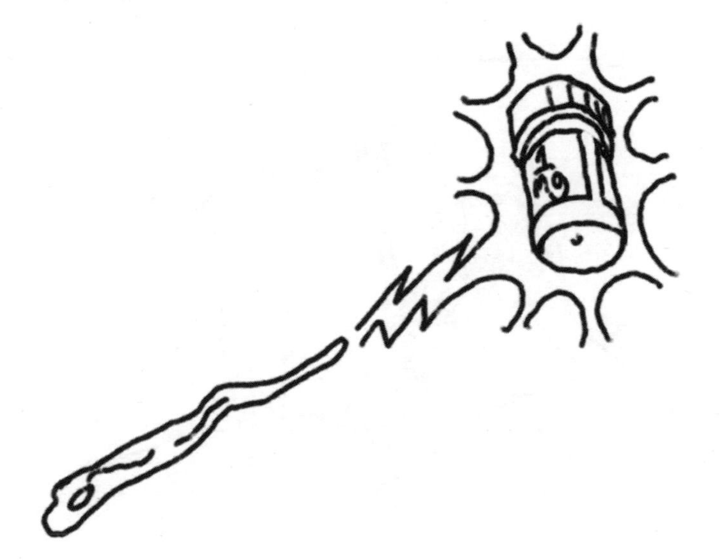

68. Benzo-trix Lestrange

Witchy, wild-eyed woman who, by shriek or by sneak, always gets her Clonazepam prescription refilled.

69. Captain ACAB (All Cetaceans are Bastards)

Straight-edge seadog with a buzzcut and eyebrow slit. Edits a zine about sperm whale violence on the Eastern sea-board. Putting together a ten-song, eleven-minute EP, whose title we can't repeat but it involves doing something terrible with a blowhole. Saving up to buy his own bass.

70. Basementus Finch

Seething actuary for Alabama cotton plantations. Campaigning to get his child's school named after Robert E. Lee.

71. Cuckleberry Finn

Sexually frustrated husband trying unsuccessfully to introduce ethical non-monogamy to Hannibal, Missouri.

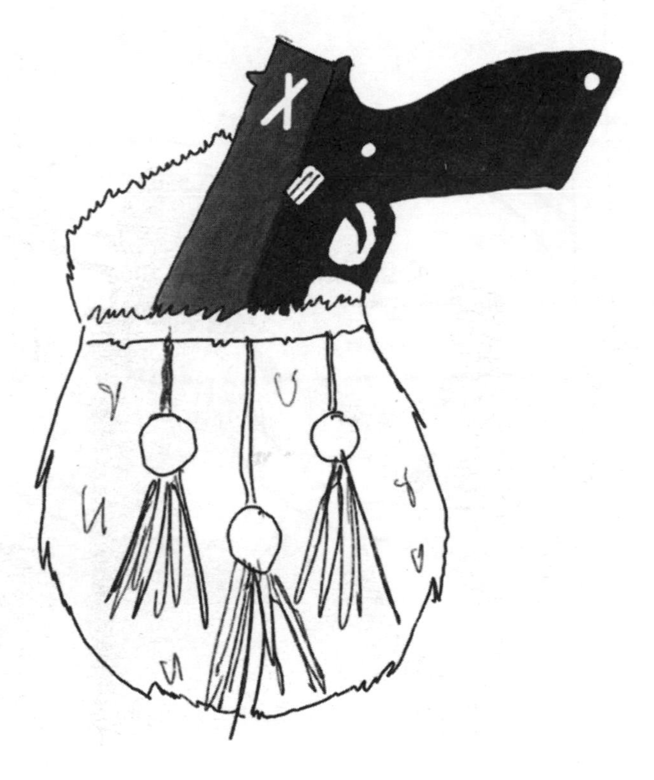

72. Jock Reacher

Effete Scot shagging his way to the top of the American intelligence establishment.

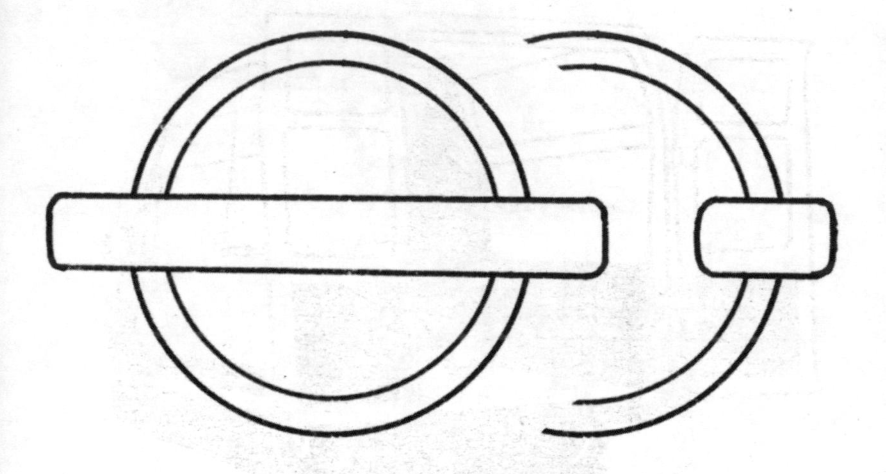

73. David Cop-a-feel

Gropey shop-floor manager of the Nissan plant in Sunderland. Banned from the Christmas party.

74. Adrianus Van Renting

Dutch doctor who needs to move a large amount of boxes. On the phone to Enterprise trying to negotiate a fair rate.

75. Clement Smith

Enthusiastic hagiographer at the Ministry of Truth.
Just happy for the opportunity.

76. Jack Reacharound

Statement from lawyers:
Mr Reacharound is a private individual.

77. The Dyspraxic of Notre Dame

Wants you to know that not all disabilities are visible, spends a lot of time justifying his blue badge while parking in priority spots. Believed to have died in the fire.

78. The Muntjac of Notre Dame

Petite, endangered deer that accidentally spent its final years trapped in a UNESCO world heritage site. Known for its guileless affection for humans and animals alike, the widely loved ungulate was barbecued to a crisp in the fire.

79. The Jack Black of Notre Dame

Iconoclastic music teacher who took flack for belfry-based hacky sac but made waves with a low-key laid-back soundtrack that's perfect for two guys having a smoke and a chat and a six pack. Incinerated along with the dyspraxic and the muntjac in the 2019 fire.

80. The Massive Attack of Notre Dame

Trip-hop group of nineties fame, who for some reason set up their studio in the belfry of a Parisian cathedral. Perished in the fire with their latest album still unfinished.

81. The Lee Myung-bak of Notre Dame

Former president of South Korea, keen on kickbacks but took immediately to the Muntjac, jammed with Jack Black and those wack sadsacks Massive Attack, called the whole thing good craic and took a different tack by setting up out back with the Muntjac till a gimcrack arson attack sent the whole wolf pack up in a smokestack.

82. The Hunchback of Tierra del Fuego

Appeared unexpectedly on the South American archipelago not long after the Notre Dame fire. Claims to have never visited Paris.

83. Short John Tungsten

Diminutive proprietor of an independent hardware store in Padstow. Gets terribly seasick.

84. TinTinTin

Third son of a distinguished Belgian crime-fighting family.

85. TinTinTinTin

Fourth son of same.

86. Tinx10^9

Youngest son of Belgian crime-fighting family.

87. Tin

The eldest.

88. Judah Ben-Him

Currently suing the Emperor Tiberius for a misgendering incident at the Circus Maximus.

89. Catpiss Everdeen

Having sought to parlay her love of animals into a bustling small enterprise after university, she found that she had completely underestimated the practical challenges of running a cat café in Stroud.

90. They-Man

Non-binary master of the universe, owner/operator of the National Trust site and wedding venue, Castle Theyskull.

91. The Divorcée of Bath

Having done very well out of recent legal proceedings, this middle-aged Pinot Grigio enthusiast lurks in the trendy cafes of the Somerset town telling hour long anecdotes about her recent forays onto Tinder.

92. Stasi Buchanan

East German spy posing as a ditzy Long Island socialite in order to extort the running dogs of Yankee capital.

93. More Than Enough William

Self-assured older brother of the popular literary schoolboy, who refuses to talk himself down.

94. Wazlan

Shaggy maned itinerant who stinks of piss and thinks he's Jesus.

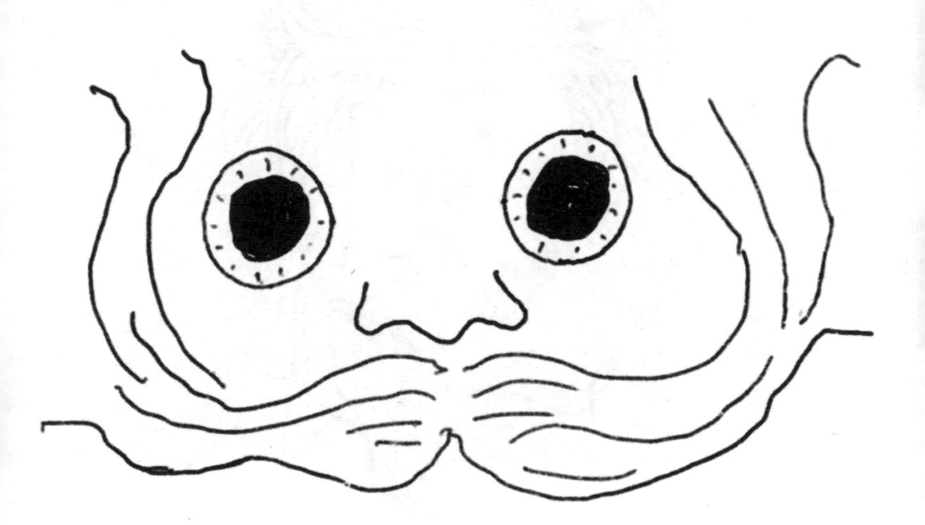

95. Trip Van Winkle

Wide eyed rave goer who feels like he's been awake for 100 years after overdosing on VK and speed.

96. Giles Cullen

Embittered hack and sad-sack who writes about tagliatelle and wanking.

97. Chip Van Winkle

Excessively sleepy purveyor of fast food, who operates a mobile bistro on the Blackpool coast. Doesn't sell winkles, is sick of people asking.

98. Sherlock Holmes

Smartarse heroin addict and parasitical bore, doomed by jealousy of his accomplished intelligence officer brother Mycroft. Dawdling in obscurity, he spent much of his life exploiting the bereavements of provincial gentry and bothering metropolitan detectives with sad-sack theories and inane conjecture. Mediocre violinist.

99. Ms. Marple

Less ambitious younger sister of elderly sleuth. Also unmarried, she channels her free time in Radio 4 and bridge, rather than investigating conspicuously prevalent murders in the village of St Mary Mead.

100. Ron Valjean

Proud and capable bread thief, still undiscovered due to enduring friendship with the local police inspector.

101. Cilla Devil

Elderly Scouse pub quiz host who, nearly 70 years later, won't stop banging on about being at school with Paul McCartney. Banned from Easyjet - and Ryanair - for acts of grotesque rudeness to their staff.

THE FENCE

CONCLUSION

As you close this book, allow Gary Potter, Euston Bear, Ms. Marple and the rest of them to get on with their quiet, largely drama-free lives. Let them go quietly into that mediocre night. Leave them to turn up at the family home at Christmas and simmer with resentment as their successful siblings regale their parents with tales of successes, leave them to bristle at every family wedding when someone asks 'and what are you doing with yourself?', leave them to very occasionally give misguided interviews about their childhood to the tabloid press when they need to raise a bit of extra cash for a foreign holiday.

Leave them, of course, until you find out you're one with them. At some point in this literary dreamscape you'll realise, as we did, that you're commuting alongside them, putting out the bins next door to them, lingering at the school gates with them as they pick up some shit literary nieces and nephews. When you do, flash them a smile of recognition; they'll like that.

So there you have it; if literature is a dream, then you can wake up now, safe in the knowledge that you stand in no way more accomplished in the field of literary knowledge than when you first picked up this book.

THE FENCE

THE FENCE